Searchlight BOOKS™

How Does Energy Work?

Investigating Electricity

Sally M. Walker

Lerner Publications Company
Minneapolis

Author's note: The experiments in this book use the metric measurement system, as that's the system most commonly used by scientists.

Lerner Publications Company
A division of Lerner Publishing Group, Inc.
241 First Avenue North
Minneapolis, MN 55401 U.S.A.

Website address: www.lernerbooks.com

Library of Congress Cataloging-in-Publication Data

Walker, Sally M.
    Investigating Electricity / by Sally M. Walker.
        p.   cm. — (Searchlight books™—how does energy work?)
    Includes index.
    ISBN 978-0-7613-5772-8 (lib. bdg. : alk. paper)
    1. Electricity—Juvenile literature. I. Title.
QC527.2 .W356 2012
537—dc22   2010035819

Manufactured in the United States of America
1 – DP – 7/15/11

Contents

Chapter 1

PEOPLE AND ELECTRICITY

Long ago, people lit their homes with candles. Now we use electricity. Electricity is a form of energy. It can be used in many ways.

How do people use electricity?

Look around you. What electrical things can you see? Lights? A computer? A TV?

Electricity powers lamps, computers, and many other things around a home.

Safety First

Electricity is helpful. But it can be dangerous! So remember these safety rules. Don't touch electrical outlets. Keep electrical wires away from water. Don't touch cracked wires. Go inside during a thunderstorm. Lightning is electricity.

Electricity is powerful. It can hurt or even kill people.

The experiments in this book are safe. But before doing them, talk with an adult. He or she might like to help you experiment.

ALL SCIENTISTS NEED TO STAY SAFE. IT'S SMART TO HAVE AN ADULT'S HELP WHEN YOU DO EXPERIMENTS.

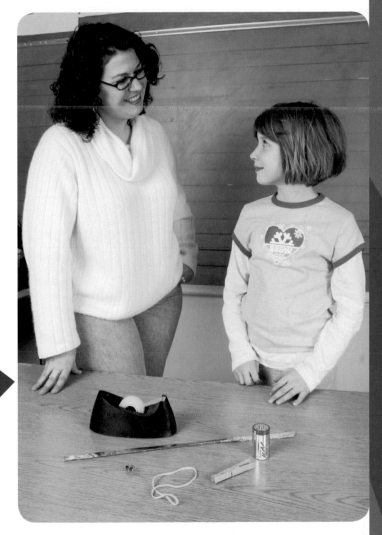

Chapter 2

AMAZING ATOMS

When you turn on a lamp, electricity lights the bulb. But where does electricity begin? It begins inside atoms. Atoms are tiny particles. They are so small you can't see them.

How does electricity make a lamp light up?

All of these things are made of atoms. Different kinds of atoms combine in different ways to make up everything we see.

Everything around you is made of atoms. There are different kinds of atoms. And they can join together in different ways. That's why we have different substances, like air, apples, and toys.

Three Parts

An atom has three parts. The parts are protons, electrons, and neutrons. Protons and electrons have electrical energy. A proton's energy is called a positive charge. An electron's energy is called a negative charge. Neutrons have no charge. The whole atom doesn't have a charge either. That's because the protons and the electrons balance each other out.

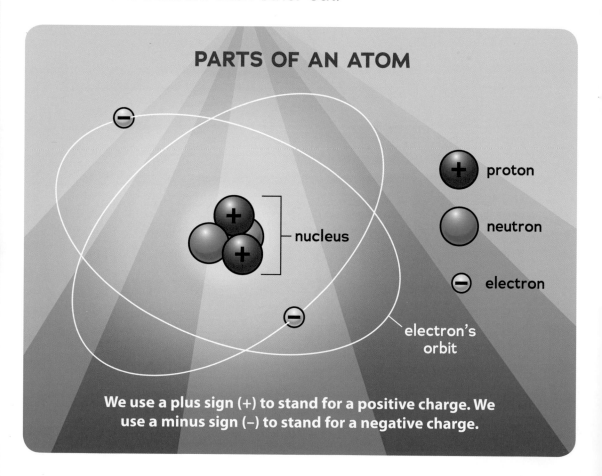

PARTS OF AN ATOM

nucleus

proton

neutron

electron

electron's orbit

We use a plus sign (+) to stand for a positive charge. We use a minus sign (–) to stand for a negative charge.

These boys and girls are standing near one another. They are like protons and neutrons crowded together in an atom's nucleus. If they are the nucleus, where would the electrons be in this picture?

Protons and neutrons are in an atom's center. This center is called the nucleus. Electrons circle around the nucleus. Their path is called an orbit. Some electrons circle close to the nucleus. Others circle farther away.

Free Electrons

Rubbing objects together can move electrons. Sometimes an electron gets knocked out of its orbit. Then it is called a free electron.

When you pet a dog, you may be moving electrons around. Rubbing the animal's fur can bump the electrons.

A free electron may jump to another atom. Atoms that gain or lose electrons become ions. An ion is an atom with an electrical charge. Ions with extra electrons have a negative charge. Ions with too few electrons have a positive charge.

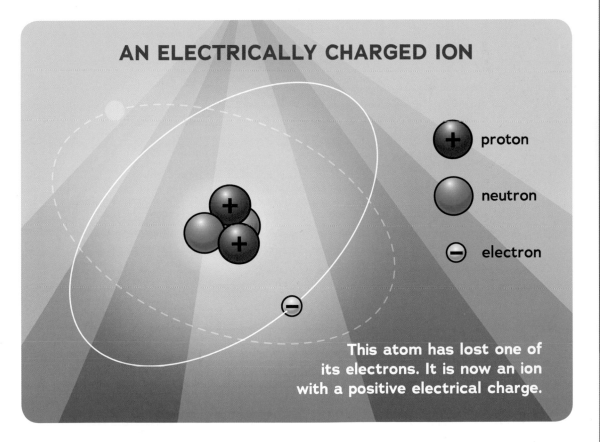

AN ELECTRICALLY CHARGED ION

proton

neutron

electron

This atom has lost one of its electrons. It is now an ion with a positive electrical charge.

Chapter 3

ELECTRIC CHARGE

Most objects have no charge. But an object can become charged when it loses or gains electrons. See for yourself.

Experiment Time!

You'll need two balloons, a sheet of paper, a 41-centimeter-long piece of string, a yardstick, a marker, and a scissors.

How can you use these simple things to make an electrical charge?

Draw several penny-sized circles on the paper. Cut the circles out. Put them on a table. Draw an *X* on each balloon. Blow up both balloons. Tie them shut.

Pick up one of the balloons. Rub the *X* against your hair fifteen times. Rubbing makes some electrons in your hair leave their orbits. These free electrons move from your hair to the balloon. The spot marked with an *X* on the balloon has extra electrons. It has a negative charge.

There are millions of electrons in every strand of your hair. Rubbing the balloon against your hair bumps those electrons.

Hold the balloon's *X* about 2.5 centimeters above the paper circles. What happens? The circles jump to the balloon. Why?

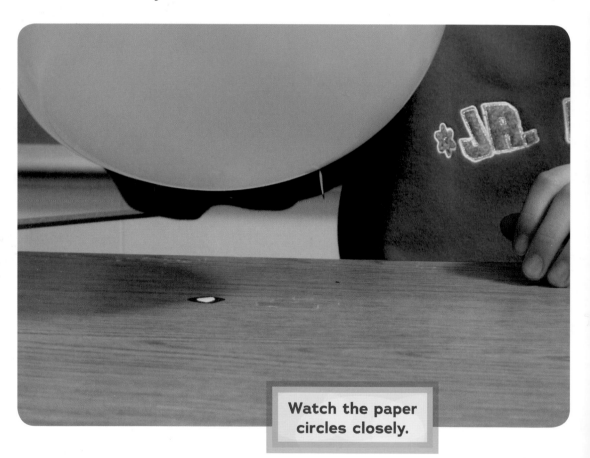

Watch the paper circles closely.

Static electricity makes the paper stick to the balloon.

Static Electricity

Static electricity holds the circles to the balloon. Static electricity is energy created between objects with different, or unlike, charges. Unlike charges pull toward each other.

The part of the balloon you marked with an *X* has a negative charge. That negative charge pulls positive charges in the circles toward the balloon. Static electricity forms. It holds the circles and the balloon together.

Two objects with the same kind of charge have like charges. Like charges push away from each other.

Prove It

Tie one end of the string around the knot of one balloon. Tie the other end around one end of the yardstick. Put the yardstick on a table so the balloon hangs down. Lift the balloon. Rub the marked *X* on your hair fifteen times. Let go of the balloon.

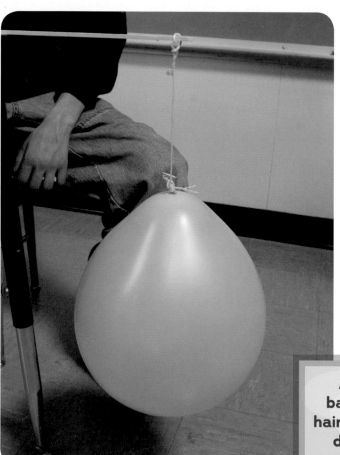

After rubbing the balloon against your hair, let it hang straight down on its string.

Pick up the other balloon. Rub its *X* on your hair fifteen times. Try to touch the *X* on this balloon to the *X* on the hanging balloon. (Don't touch the hanging balloon with your hand.) What happens? The *X* on the hanging balloon moves away from the balloon in your hand. Why? Both balloons have a negative charge. Like charges push away from each other.

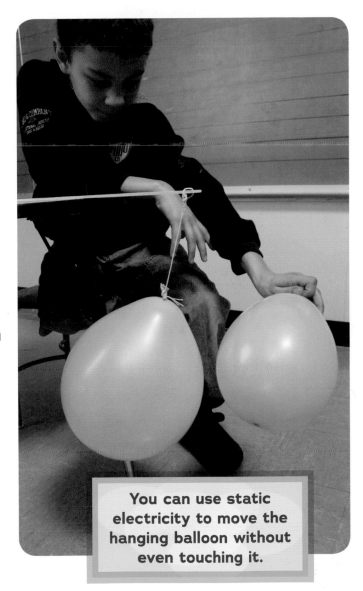

You can use static electricity to move the hanging balloon without even touching it.

Chapter 4

CURRENTS AND CIRCUITS

Static electricity lasts only a short time. It needs more free electrons to last. When you stopped rubbing the balloon on your hair, free electrons stopped moving to the balloon. That meant the static electricity stopped too. But if electrons keep moving to the balloon, electricity can last. A steady flow of free electrons is called a current.

Static electricity can make your hair stand up like this, but only for a little while. Why doesn't static electricity last very long?

Current moves when free electrons from one atom pass to the next. Let's see how this works. Stand in a row with your friends. Whisper a word to the person next to you. If everyone whispers the word to the next person, the word reaches the end of the line. Current flows along a wire the same way. The wire's atoms stay in place as the free electrons flow from one atom to the next.

No one moves out of place in your line. But the word you whisper moves from person to person. This is how electricity moves too.

Conductors

Current flows easily through some materials. These materials are called conductors. Silver and copper are conductors.

This copper wire is a good conductor. It carries electric current well.

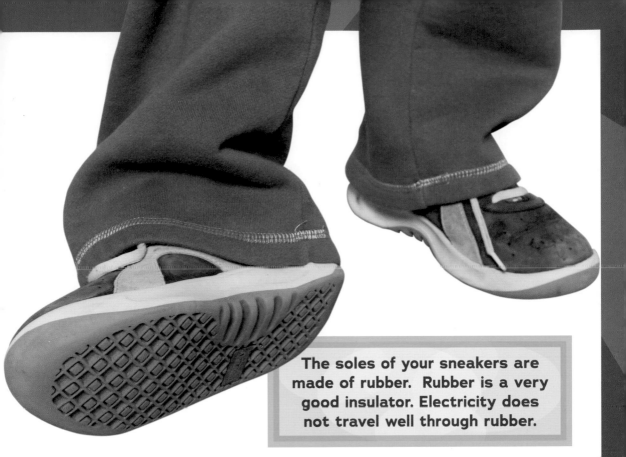

The soles of your sneakers are made of rubber. Rubber is a very good insulator. Electricity does not travel well through rubber.

Insulators

Some materials don't carry current well. These materials are called insulators. Wood and rubber are insulators. An insulator can protect you from getting a shock. Rubber is wrapped around wires to keep their current from hurting people.

What Makes a Current?

You made static electricity when you rubbed a balloon against your hair. But where does a current come from?

Putting certain materials together can make a current. These materials are inside batteries. They make electricity inside the battery.

Batteries come in all shapes and sizes. What have you used batteries for? A flashlight? A video game?

You can use a battery to make a current flow. You'll need a size D battery, a flashlight bulb, a clothespin, clear tape, and a sheet of aluminum foil.

HOW CAN THESE THINGS MAKE ELECTRICITY FLOW? FIND OUT!

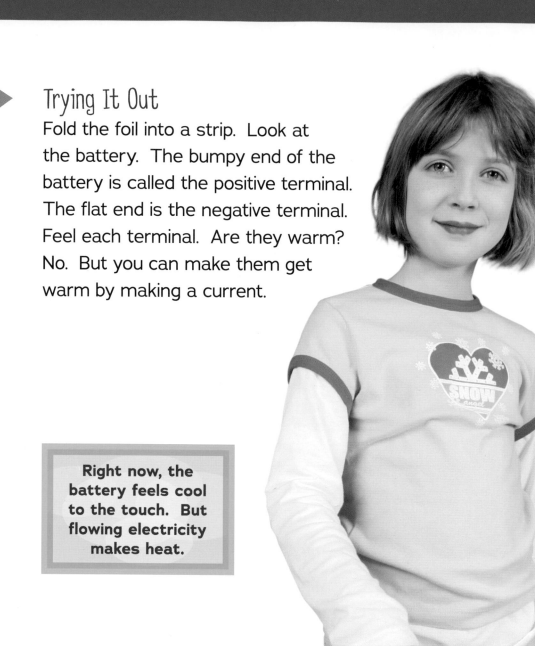

Trying It Out

Fold the foil into a strip. Look at the battery. The bumpy end of the battery is called the positive terminal. The flat end is the negative terminal. Feel each terminal. Are they warm? No. But you can make them get warm by making a current.

Right now, the battery feels cool to the touch. But flowing electricity makes heat.

Tape one end of the foil strip across the negative terminal. Did the terminal feel warm? No. Hold the other end of the foil across the positive terminal. Are the terminals getting warm? Yes. That's because current is flowing. Currents make heat.

The battery should not get warm enough to hurt you. But if it does feel too warm, just set it down!

The current flowed because you made a path for it to follow. This path is called a circuit. Electricity needs a circuit to flow. The circuit must connect the battery's positive and negative terminals. The circuit must also be closed. A closed circuit is a path without spaces in it.

Closed and Open Circuits

Use one hand to make a circle with your thumb and index finger. Can you trace all the way around the circle with the index finger of your other hand? Yes! Your fingers make a closed circuit.

Holding your fingers in an OK sign can help you think about what a closed circuit looks like. Your fingers make a complete loop.

Spread your thumb and index finger apart. This time, there's a space between your fingers. You can't trace a complete circle. Your fingers don't make a closed circuit.

Hold your fingers apart. They do not make a complete loop. There is a gap, or space. There is also a gap in circuits that are not closed.

Closing a Circuit

Look at your battery and the foil strip. One end of the strip is taped to the negative terminal. The other end is not touching the positive terminal. You can't trace along the foil from one terminal to the other without lifting your finger. It isn't a closed circuit. How could you close the circuit?

The foil is not making a complete circuit. The loop does not go all the way from the negative terminal to the positive terminal. Electricity cannot travel through the strip.

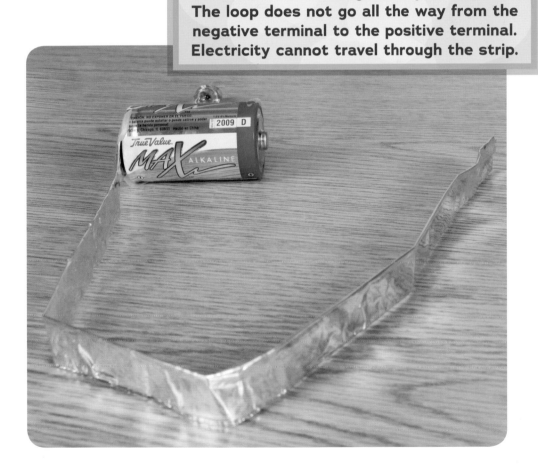

Hold the loose end of the foil against the positive terminal. Can you trace along the foil from one terminal to the other without lifting your finger? Yes. You have made a closed circuit. You know this because the terminals are warm. That means current is flowing. Current flows only through a closed circuit.

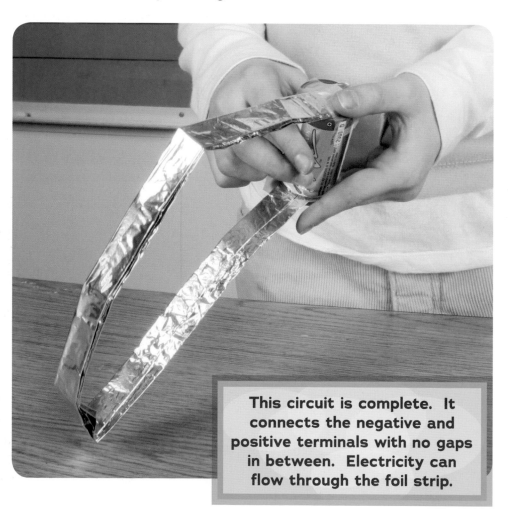

This circuit is complete. It connects the negative and positive terminals with no gaps in between. Electricity can flow through the foil strip.

Currents on the Move

To flow, a current needs a closed circuit. But what makes the current move? Free electrons need a push to get moving. That push comes from electrical force. Electrical force is measured in volts. Your battery has 1.5 volts. That's enough force to push electrical charges along the foil.

Look for the word *volts* or the letter *V* on your battery. Every battery has a certain number of volts. The more volts a battery has, the more of a "push" it can give to an electric current.

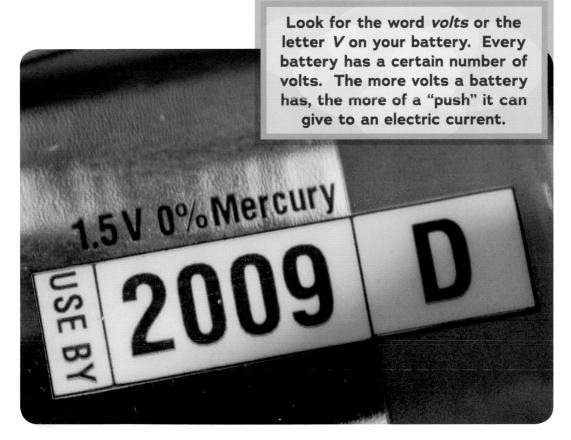

Volts force current to keep flowing. Flowing current will light your flashlight bulb. But to do this, you need a closed circuit.

Experiment Time Again!

Wrap the loose end of the foil around the metal part of the bulb. Clamp the foil in place with the clothespin. Make sure the other end of the foil is taped to the negative terminal.

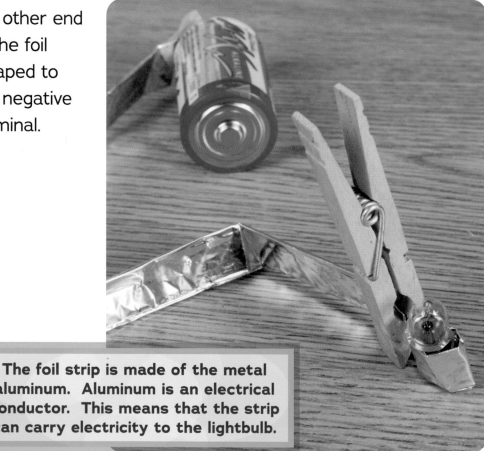

The foil strip is made of the metal aluminum. Aluminum is an electrical conductor. This means that the strip can carry electricity to the lightbulb.

Does the bulb light if you touch the contact to the side of the battery? No, because the battery is covered in plastic. Plastic is an insulator.

The metal point on the bottom of the bulb is called the contact. The metal contact is a good conductor.

Touch the bulb's contact to the negative terminal on the battery. The terminal's metal also is a good conductor. Does the bulb light? No. It doesn't light because the negative terminal is not connected to the positive terminal. You haven't made a closed circuit yet.

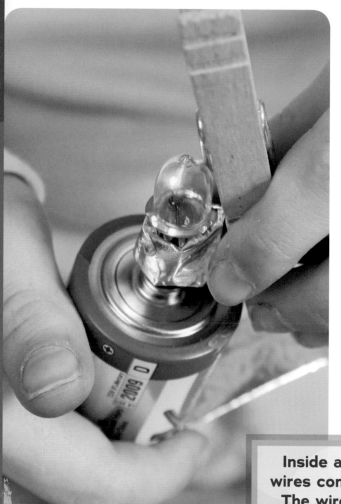

Touch the contact to the positive terminal. Does the bulb light? Yes! The circuit is closed. Current flows from the negative terminal. It flows through the foil to the bulb and then on to the positive terminal. The circuit is complete. Current flows through the wires inside the bulb and makes it light up.

Inside a lightbulb are two straight wires connected by a thin, curly wire. The wire glows and the bulb lights up when the circuit is complete.

Electricity is useful for running machines and making heat. It can also make light. And that's useful for reading a book at night!

Next time you read by a lamp, think about how electricity works!

Glossary

atom: a very tiny particle that makes up all things

charge: the energy of an atom or part of an atom. When atoms gain or lose electrons, they gain a charge.

circuit: the path that an electric current follows

conductor: a material that carries electric current well

current: the flow of electricity through something

electron: the part of an atom that has a negative charge. Electrons circle around the center of the atom.

insulator: a material that does not carry electric current well

ion: an atom that has gained or lost electrons

negative charge: the charge that a substance has if its atoms have gained extra electrons from other atoms

nucleus: the center of an atom. The nucleus is made of protons and neutrons.

orbit: a circular or oval path. Electrons follow an orbit around the center of an atom.

particle: a tiny piece

positive charge: the charge that a substance has if its atoms have lost electrons to other atoms

static electricity: energy created between objects that have different electric charges

terminal: one of the ends of a battery. Every battery has a positive terminal and a negative terminal.

Learn More about Electricity

Books

Jango-Cohen, Judith. *Ben Franklin's Big Shock*. Minneapolis: Millbrook Press, 2006. Learn all about Ben Franklin's interest in and experiments with electricity.

Moore, Rob. *Why Does Electricity Flow?: All about Electricity*. New York: PowerKids Press, 2010. This engaging book explores science mysteries related to electricity.

Spilsbury, Richard. *What Is Electricity and Magnetism?: Exploring Science with Hands-On Activities*. Berkeley Heights, NJ: Enslow Elementary, 2008. Check out this title to find more electricity experiments you can try.

Waring, Geoff. *Oscar and the Bird: A Book about Electricity*. Cambridge, MA: Candlewick Press, 2009. Waring takes a playful look at electricity.

Websites

Enchanted Learning: Static Electricity
http://www.enchantedlearning.com/physics/Staticelectricity.shtml
Read up on static electricity at this page from Enchanted Learning.

Energy Kids: History of Energy
http://www.eia.doe.gov/kids/energy.cfm?page=4
This website from the Energy Information Administration has timelines exploring important discoveries about energy.

The NASA SciFiles: Electricity Activities
http://scifiles.larc.nasa.gov/text/kids/D_Lab/acts_electric.html
This NASA site features several fun activities for learning about electricity.

Index

Photo Acknowledgments

Photographs copyright © Andy King. Additional images in this book are used with the permission of: © Jack Hollingsworth/Getty Images, p. 5; © Wolfe Larry/Shutterstock Images, p. 6; © Laura Westlund/Independent Picture Service, pp. 10, 13.

Front Cover: © Todd Strand/Independent Picture Service.

Main body text set in Adrianna Regular 14/20.
Typeface provided by Chank.